Those Aren't Pillows!
A Fan's Guide to Planes, Trains and Automobiles

Those Aren't Pillows!
A Fan's Guide to Planes, Trains and Automobiles

A catalogue record for this book is available from the British Library

ISBN 978-1-9996533-4-7

Design by Gary McGarvey youresomehorse.com

Edited by Joe Shooman joeshooman.com

Printed and bound by Kindle Direct Publishing

www.searchingforcandy.com

Dedicated to the memory of my friend, Patty Ferraro.
I'm so sorry I never made it to Chicago in time.

Contents

Introduction

Do you remember the first time you watched *Planes, Trains and Automobiles*? If it didn't make you cry with laughter and weep like a baby I'm not sure this book is for you. In fact, if you don't still get that reaction (on at least a yearly basis), maybe you need to get your heart and head checked out?

By John Hughes, this masterpiece was originally written in just over a weekend, but 'masterpiece' is an understatement. It was inspired by a true-life travel disaster that Hughes experienced himself. Hughes went on what was meant to be a one day trip from Chicago to New York, returning the same day, but his flight was diverted to Wichita and he got home five days later.

Planes, Trains and Automobiles is a classic that everyone loves. It gets played repeatedly every year, especially around American Thanksgiving as the film sees one of the main characters struggling to get home for the holidays.

The film shows strangers from worlds apart coming together (even if one is reluctant). The casting and writing could not have been more perfect, with co-leads Steve Martin and John Candy acting their hearts out, making you laugh and cry with just the lift of an eyebrow or the squeeze of a red mitten.

This book is for those fans of the film, so if you have not watched it previously, please put this down and go and watch it first. I don't want to spoil the movie for anyone, plus this book will make a hell of a lot more sense if you are familiar with the subject. If you truly thought that this was a book about Planes, Trains and Automobiles, I'm sorry, you need to go and look in the mechanical and automotive section.

I'm sure you can probably quote many quotes, if not the script verbatim, but just in case, here is a tiny recap (although we will be going through the film step by step throughout)...

Neal Page (Steve Martin) is a Madison Square Advertising Executive trying to get home to Chicago from New York just days before Thanksgiving. Neal is plagued by circumstances, weather and, from the cab scene onwards, Shower Curtain Ring Salesman, Del Griffith (John Candy). His plans to get home are repeatedly dashed by a series of unforeseen events.

The Director

Planes, Trains and Automobiles was originally going to be directed by Howard Deutch (*Pretty In Pink*) as Hughes was just finishing up on *She's Having a Baby*. However, when Steve Martin signed up to do the film, writer John Hughes decided he wanted to work with Martin. He swapped with Deutch who then directed another Hughes movie, *The Great Outdoors*, which was filmed the following year with John Candy and Dan Aykroyd.

John Hughes

There are many words to describe John Hughes, 'genius' is the one that gets bandied around a lot and he is most certainly worthy of that title. A prolific writer and director of some of the most iconic movies of the 1980s and 90s, his resume boasts *Sixteen Candles*, *Ferris Bueller's Day Off*, *Weird Science*, *Pretty In Pink*, *The Breakfast Club*, *The Great Outdoors*, *Home Alone*, *Uncle Buck*, and of course, *Planes, Trains and Automobiles*.

Born on 18th February 1950 in Lansing, Michigan, USA, John Wilden Hughes Jr was originally in advertising, before becoming an author of humorous essays and stories for the *National Lampoon*. In fact, it was here where he would make his first film, *National Lampoon's Vacation*.

Hughes was integral to the careers of those considered 'The Brat Pack' in the 80s - Molly Ringwald, Anthony Michael Hall, Judd Nelson, Ally Sheedy, Judd Nelson, Demi Moore, Rob Lowe, Emilio Estevez and Andrew McCarthy, as well as Matthew Broderick, Macaulay Culkin and writer/director, Christopher Columbus. Hughes was best known for his coming-of-age teen movies although he would branch out later on. Hughes had a magnificent ability to capture the human element, distil it and project it onto the screen and rebound it into our hearts, idiosyncrasies and all. A prolific writer, he would often write film scripts in a weekend as he needed to type as fast as the dialogue would come to him. He liked to work that way so he could see if he liked the idea before doing multiple, usually 25-30, rewrites.

Paul Hirsch, an award-winning editor in Hollywood, worked with Hughes and described him in his book, *A Long Time Ago In a Cutting Room Far, Far away….,* Hirsch wrote, *"I think of him as a skilled miniaturist, who could take a simple situation and from it weave endlessly elaborate and hilarious complications."*.

During Hughes' career he would feature John Candy in more of his films than any other actor, however before working on *Planes, Trains and Automobiles* they had only met once before. After *Planes, Trains and Automobiles* they would become best friends. Candy initially featured in *National Lampoon's Vacation*, then later *She's Having a Baby*, *The Great Outdoors*, *Uncle Buck*, *Home Alone* and *Career Opportunities,* as well as *Only the Lonely* produced by Hughes Productions. There were also rumours that Hughes had written and was going to be directing a film starring Candy and Sly Stallone, a comedy titled *Bartholomew vs. Neff.* Due to be filmed Summer '94 in the Chicago suburbs, Stallone was going to play a former professional baseball player who lived next door to corporate guy Candy chronicling their friendship.

After Candy passed away in 1994, Hughes practically retired from Hollywood and stepped away from the public eye.

On 5th August 2009, Hughes was in New York City with his wife, Nancy, visiting his son James and their new grandson. Whilst taking a walk, Hughes suffered a massive heart attack, was rushed to hospital but sadly could not be saved. In 2019 his wife, Nancy passed away. Hughes is survived by his sons, John Hughes lll, James Hughes, his grandchildren and of course all those timeless classics he wrote and directed.

The Leading Co-Stars

Steve Martin

Stephen Glenn Martin was born 14th August 1945 in Waco, Texas, and raised in Inglewood, California.

Martin's first-ever job was at Disneyland, selling guidebooks at weekends and school holidays, and he also spent a lot of his time at the Main Street Magic Shop. After High School, Martin attended Santa Ana College where he studied drama and English poetry. It was around this time he started to participate in performances, productions and comedies at The Bird Cage Theater where he would eventually join a comedy troupe at Knott's Berry Farm. Martin would enrol as a major in philosophy and was heading to become a professor, before swapping his major to theater. In the evenings he would work in local clubs, and he would finally drop out of college at the age of 21.

Martin was a keen writer, and in 1967 a girlfriend at the time was working on *The Smothers Brothers Comedy Hour*. She gave some of Martin's work to the head writer, who then employed him out of his own pocket. By 1969 Martin and the other writers won an Emmy for their work.

During the 70s Martin found himself doing a plethora of appearances as a standup comedian, including *The Tonight Show Starring Johnny Carson*, *The Gong Show*, *The Muppet Show* and *Saturday Night Live* (in fact Martin was one of the most successful hosts of *SNL* ever). As well as these show appearances he released several comedy albums including *A Wild and Crazy Guy* (1978) and had the following a rockstar would be proud of, selling out large venues filled with screaming fans. However for Martin, it wasn't his ambition to be a stand-up, he wanted to be in the movies!

Martin's first small film role would be in 1972, *Another Fine Mess*. With a few other film roles under his belt, it was really in

1979 when he starred in *The Jerk* that Martin's film career was put firmly on the map. *The Jerk*, directed by comedy royalty, Carl Reiner, had a budget of US$4 million and grossed around US$100 million at the box office. Films considered classics, continued with *Dead Men Don't Wear Plaid* (1982), *The Man With Two Brains* (1983) and *The Three Amigos* (1986) in which he co-starred with Chevy Chase and Martin Short.

Of course, in 1987 he would star alongside John Candy in *Planes, Trains and Automobiles*, followed later that year by *Roxanne* and then *Dirty Rotten Scoundrels* (1988).

Martin's acting career would stay strong right through the 90s. However in the 00s, he put Hollywood on more of the backburner whilst he focused on writing, including his autobiography *Born Standing Up* and focusing on his love of the banjo as a professional musician, collaborating with *The Steep Canyon Rangers* and Edie Brickell. Martin is also touring with his old friend, Martin Short, all over the world with their comedy show.

John Candy

Born on Halloween 31st October 1950, John Candy (how funny he should be born on a day when people give candy away) was born in Newmarket, Ontario, moving to East York when he was five years old after his dad passed away.

Candy fell into acting and comedy after studying journalism at Centennial College, before swapping to acting. Originally he'd tried to apply to join the Marines in Buffalo, however, due to an old knee injury he wasn't accepted. That knee also blew any career in football Candy was heading for.

A lover of TV and film, John was never told as a kid he was going to be on TV, but only that he'd turn into one if he didn't stop watching it. After working various jobs including a part-time sales assistant, a greeting card salesman and an usher at this local movie theater, The Donlands, Candy first got his first acting break in adverts and children's theater. It was here he would meet Valri Bromfield, comedy partner of Dan Aykroyd at that time. Bromfield and Aykroyd tricked Candy into auditioning for *Second City* in 1973. Candy first joined *Second City Chicago* where he learnt alongside the likes of Bill Murray, before going back to perform with the Toronto troupe. After the success of *Saturday Night Live*, *Second City* bosses were concerned that they would lose all their talent to TV, so they started *SCTV* (Second City TV) a sketch-based show based around a fictional TV station. Alongside Harold Ramis, Dave Thomas, Catherine O'Hara, Joe Flaherty, Eugene Levy, Andrea Martin and later, Rick Moranis and Martin Short, they found screen fame and Hollywood started to call.

Candy would eventually go on to become a bona fide movie star, from his humble beginnings in Stephen Spielberg's *1941*, to playing Tom Hanks' brother in *Splash*, he would then turn movie critics heads when showing his full range as Del in *Planes, Trains and Automobiles*. Candy would go on to star in so many films that are still loved today, *Home Alone*, *The Great*

Outdoors, *Cool Runnings*, *Spaceballs* and, of course, he's still everyone's favourite uncle in *Uncle Buck*.

From 1991-94 Candy also co-owned The Toronto Argonauts with Bruce McNall and hockey superstar, Wayne Gretzky. Candy practically single-handedly rejuvenated the Canadian Football League in 1991, where incidentally the Argos would also go on to win The Grey Cup that year.

As mentioned in John Hughes' section, we sadly lost Candy to a heart attack on 4th March 1994, whilst he was in Durango, Mexico, filming the spoof western, *Wagons East!* At just the tender age of just 43, Candy left us too soon and boy this world needs him now more than ever. Luckily for us, he left a plethora of work that we love and enjoy to this day, and that, that kind of makes him immortal.

Candy is survived by his widow, Rosemary, his children Jennifer and Chris and his grandchild, Finley.

Flying By the Seat of Their Pants

In 1987, the year PTA was filmed and released, The Directors Guild of America (DGA) were due to strike, so all filming had to be finished by 30th June, ready for strike day. If that didn't put enough pressure on the picture, they also fell behind schedule. By the end of filming Hughes had actually used twice the industry average of film reel. They were all working 14-hour days and were so behind that at some point Candy and Martin agreed not to ad-lib anymore and just follow the script to keep things moving. On top of that, before the filming had even finished they had the movie booked into thousands of theaters on 9th November '87 ready for the Thanksgiving build-up, however, in the end, it wasn't actually released until 25th November '87.

The DGA, whose purpose as a labor union is to provide support services and benefits to its members, wanted to ensure that film and television directors are credited for their work as well as advocating better working conditions. They wanted to shut down Hollywood to negotiate 'final cut' rights, so directors could have the final approval on a film. The strike was against Columbia Pictures, Warner Bros and the NBC-TV Network. In actual fact, the whole strike - expected to last months - only lasted three hours and five minutes before the networks relented! It is the shortest Hollywood strike in history.

The Journey - step by step...

Two Days Before Thanksgiving

Location: Office, 767 5th Avenue, Manhattan.

The film starts with Advertising Executive Neal Page in a boardroom with several other men and a female secretary, watching the head honcho painfully pondering over some marketing stills. The office is actually in The General Motors Building, a 705ft tower on Fifth Avenue, Manhattan. The boardroom is quiet, tense almost. Neal is visibly concerned as he needs to get to the airport for 6pm to make sure he gets home to his family in Chicago for Thanksgiving.

On first impressions, it is clear that Neal works hard and follows the rules, and he expects everyone to do the same. His wife and kids wait dutifully in their large family home in Chicago, for their dad often works away. From the outside, it looks like Neal has his life together, a good job and picture-perfect home life. He wears suits, takes care of his health and in the main, will look after himself to get to where he wants to be.

The meeting overruns and just as he gets near the elevator he realises he's forgotten his gloves, he decides he doesn't need them as he'll go from the lobby to the taxi cab, to the airport, to the aeroplane and then home - oh how wrong he is! Neal asks his colleague, John, who is travelling on a later flight to grab them for him, John, is played by Lyman Ward (who also played Ferris Bueller's dad) warns him that he'll never make it in time. As Neal gets outside it is rush hour and he joins the proverbial rat-race to win a taxi cab.

Location: Park Avenue at 52nd Street Manhattan, NYC
During the time they were filming *Planes, Trains and Automobiles*, Hughes was just finishing filming *She's Having a Baby* starring Kevin Bacon and Elizabeth McGovern. As with

many of Hughes' films, he builds a universe and very often will use the same actors and have those universes overlapping. The characters he creates pretty much live in similar areas, for example, the Pages in *PTA* live one town over from the McCallisters in *Home Alone*, and they live around the corner from The Russells in *Uncle Buck*. So it's not surprising that Page has to race Kevin Bacon (potentially as his character in *She's Having a Baby*) after they both make eye contact and realised it is a war to get a taxi, down Park Avenue at 54th and 53rd Street Manhattan for a cab.

After dodging and overcoming many obstacles, sadly for Neal, he inevitably loses the race when he trips over a large trunk that someone has lazily left in his way.

As he's picking himself up he sees what turns out to be a ruthless attorney hailing a cab. As it pulls over Neal tries his luck by asking him if he can appeal to his better nature and take his cab so he doesn't miss his flight. The attorney haggles his way up to Neal paying him 75 dollars to give him the cab, meanwhile, the taxi driver is helping someone lift the trunk that had just sent Neal flying into the back of the car. As soon as Neal finishes negotiating he goes to get in the cab but it drives off before he can.

The camera pans in on the puddle where the cab has been. A single shower curtain ring is floating in it.

Incensed, Neal chases the cab through the traffic on foot! At one stage he manages to catch up with the cab and open the door, which the shocked passenger closes again as the cab drives off. Neal's briefcase gets run over.

Deleted Scenes and Script Changes
In the final shooting script, there is already some foreshadowing that Neal will be in trouble if he doesn't make it home on time. His colleague John tells Neal that he'll never

make his flight in time and tries to persuade him that a few hours difference is nothing, "What's the point of breaking your balls rushing for a six o'clock plane? Why don't you go out with me on the eight-fifteen?" Neal has to explain that he told Susan he'd be home by nine and that his excuses to Susan don't work anymore.

During the cab scene, just before Neal manages to catch up with it, we get an introduction to Del Griffith, eating beef jerky and saying to the taxi driver, "Don't give me that 'Triborough Bridge is faster' baloney. I've been to this town quite a few times. There isn't a cabbie in the Big Apple that can beat me on a fare".

I Knew I Knew Ya

Location: LaGuardia Airport, Grand Central Pkwy, East Elmhurst, New York.

Now although Neal's ticket states he is flying from JFK Airport, the scenes were filmed at LaGuardia Airport.

Neal thinks he's made it with minutes to spare when he sees that his flight is delayed.

The film cuts to Neal's family, Susan, his wife, and three kids all around the dinner table.

Back to the airport waiting lounge, Neal clocks the shocked passenger/cab stealer sitting opposite him.

Enter Del Griffith…
Del Griffith is a sweetheart of a man, warm smile, bumbling, possibly a little annoying but kind of worldly-wise. You would never imagine someone would be so successful selling shower curtain rings, but not only does Del make a living he also gets to travel all over the US, in the universe of the film it seems he has contacts all over the country from his plastic hoops. Griffith is a loud but jovial, smoking, open book (or so we think).

(The following is an excerpt from *Planes, Trains and Automobiles*)

Del: I know you, don't I? I'm usually very good with names, but I'll be damned if I haven't
*   forgotten yours.*
Neal: You stole my cab.
Del: (Chuckling) I've never stolen anything in my life!
Neal: I hailed a cab on Park Avenue this afternoon, and er, before   I   could   get   in   it,   you stole   it.

Del: (Thinks) You're the guy who tried to get my cab! I knew
I knew you. Yeah. (Chuckling)
         You scared the bejesus out of me. (Pauses and thinks)
         Come to think of it, it was awful easy getting a cab
         during rush hour.
Neal: Forget it.
Del: I can't forget it. I am sorry. I had no idea that was your
cab. Let me make it up to you
         somehow huh, please? How about a nice hot dog and a
beer?
Neal: Uh, no, thanks.
Del: Just a hot dog, then?
Neal: I'm kind of picky about what I eat.
Del: Some coffee?
Neal: No.
Del: Milk?
Neal: No.
Del: Soda?
Neal: No.
Del: Some tea?
Neal: No.
Del: Lifesavers? Slurpee?
Neal: Sir, please.
Del: Just let me know. I'm here. (Excitedly waving his
finger) I knew I knew you!

The book Del is reading is a pornographic novel, *The Canadian
Mounted*, a book solely made for the film. Sadly it doesn't
actually exist, the only other copy belongs to Deadpool (see
Deadpool 2, Ryan Reynolds is a huge Candy fan).

Deleted scenes and script changes
Before we get to this stage in the movie there are scenes that
didn't make it into the final cut, showing Neal ringing home and
going through security.

When he calls home to tell Susan his flight has been delayed
she takes the words right out of his mouth and says to him, "I

know you can't prevent flight delays. You CAN prevent travelling immediately before a holiday. I asked you not to but you had your priorities", showing that already there is some trouble at home brewing.

As for the security scene, this extract is taken from a script revision on 22 May '86.

Neal: What's the problem for God's sake?
The woman in front of him turns around, glad to share her anger.
Woman: Some jerk's been up there for ten minutes.

INT. LOBBY TICKET COUNTER
A harried female ticket agent is tapping on her computer keys.

Agent: Smoking or non-smoking?

The guy who took Neal's cab is the jerk that's been taking ten minutes.

Del (To himself): Smoking or non?
Del (To the agent): I'm trying to quit so sometimes I like non-smoking because it forces me to lay off the butts but then if we hit weather and I get shaky, I like to smoke.
Agent: (Sighs) Smoking or non-smoking?
Del: (He thinks, clicks his tongue.) Can I get an aisle set in the last row of the non-smoking section so that if I change my mind I can ask someone to switch? If you don't have an aisle, I'll take a window but if all you have are middle seats, I'll go non-smoking because if I don't have enough elbow room I cheese everybody off reaching for my smokes. Also, is this a dinner flight? But before you answer, let me say that I noticed you're wearing a wedding ring and I just want to say that your husband is a very lucky man and your perfume is heavenly.
(He smiles warmly).
As soon as Page gets through the ticket counter he runs down the corridors only to be stopped in his tracks by yet another

queue, this time at security. Of course, the delay is once again Del Griffith, emptying his pockets of anything metal as he keeps setting off the metal detectors. In the end, he realises it was a shoehorn stuck in his shoe - to him, it makes sense, his foot has been hurting him all day.

It's at this point in the previous script that Neal recognizes him as the man who stole his cab.

Another deleted scene that would have proved to be hilarious, Neal has fallen asleep in the airport lobby chair, when he wakes up he notices Del has gone, just some rubbish remains, cigarette butts, drink cups, a worn pair of Dr Scholl's foot pads, candy wrappers, a newspaper etc.

Neal decides to go to the restroom where he hears a loud whistling. Del is standing at the restroom sink in his undershirt and is shaving. He looks around and sees Neal, and greets him with "Howdy traveller!" Neal gives him a half-hearted smile and goes to the urinal. Del launches into a kind of one-way chat.

Del: On the road quite a bit? I am. I know these airlines like the back of my hand. An hour delay means an hour and a half. Your nickel against my nuts, it's snowing in Chi-town. It's the damn lake. All that... moisture. Chicago goes and the whole national air transportation system takes a dump. If you told me it was raining rabbit pellets in Chicago, I'd believe you. Bad weather town. Great pizza, the best hot dogs in the world, great parks. Damn nice zoo. Good aquarium, excellent art museum, although I've never been there personally. Knowledgeable cab drivers. Good newspapers. Nice hotels. A bit high priced but comfortable. You enjoy blues music? Blues? You like the blues?

Del, with disappointment in his face, then realises Neal has left.

Is This a Coincidence or What?

Poor Neal's bad luck doesn't stop there. As he eventually boards the delayed flight he is told that he's been booked onto coach instead of first-class, and although he argues with the stewardess he loses yet another battle and makes his way to his assigned seat, a middle seat, next to an elderly gentleman (in one of the scripts this gentleman was going to be a mum with a crying baby) and luckily for Neal, on the aisle seat, a familiar face: Del Griffith.

Already pissed off, Neal says nothing.

Del introduces himself, "Del Griffith, American Light and Fixture, Director of Sales, Shower Curtain Ring Division. I sell shower curtain rings, best in the world. And you are?"...

Neal introduces himself with hesitancy, excuses himself by saying he's not much of a conversationalist and he wants to finish the article he is reading.

Meanwhile, in O'Hare Airport Chicago, the flight announcement boards show that every flight arrival is cancelled. There is a scene that shows the aeroplane in the storm. This was actually borrowed footage, taken from the 1980 film, *Airplane*, also produced by Paramount.

Deleted scenes and script revisions

In the final shooting script, originally Neal was to find his seat between an elderly lady and a young schoolgirl. However, within seconds the stewardess realises the young girl is in the wrong seat and moves her, enter Del Griffith. Now, of course, the final script doesn't mean they kept to script, Hughes' love of improvisation meant that they filmed each scene several times in several different ways, hence the changes (so there's probably more, but without access to the rushes it's not possible to say what else was recorded).

In one of the scripts, Del asks Neal what he does, Neal says "Marketing", and that sets Del off at a tangent...

Del: "Advertising? Super. I love advertising. I do a little of that myself. I do a little of that game myself. Not officially. I help our customers with suggestions for their advertisements in trade journals and whatnot. If you've got a shower curtain in your home, there's a fifty per cent chance that the rings holding it up were sold to your supplier by me, myself and I. I like to kid people that if it weren't for me and American Light and Fixture and the shower ring division, Janet Leigh probably wouldn't have caught her lunch in Psycho. You see that flick?

Neal: (nods yes)

Del: "I like to joke but that one was no joke. I was new to the business when that baby hit the silver screen and that shower murder left a crap stain on the reputation of shower curtains the size of Texas. Pebble glass shower doors took a big bite out of our sales for several years.

"We're back on our feet now. We're doing good. The young people going into their first homes don't have the same phobia about showers that their parents had. That Alfred Hitchcock. You know what that 'Birds' film did to parakeet sales? El Dumpo, Jack. El Dumpo. Good friend of mine lost his shirt. You use curtains or doors in your home?"

Neal: (stares at him)

Del: Doors? Hell, it's no sweat off my back. I'm just happy to have someone to talk to. I finished my book about an hour ago. Filthy god darn thing. When you travel as much as I do, you run out of reading material. If it's been published, I've read it. Fiction, nonfiction, the classics. Robbins, Krantz, Hailey, Spillane. You name it. I've read it. I got so hard up last week on a layover in Atlanta, I read a biography of Prince. That's not his real name, by the way. It's Rogers Nelson."

In another version, Del takes out a company calendar and shows Neal a busty looking lady holding shower curtain rings in the shower and forces him to have a copy. The busty looking lady was actor Debra Lamb, we'll mention Lamb later too.

It's at this stage in the alternate script Neal tells Del he's not much of a conversationalist, but Del doesn't stop there and he precedes to tell Neal how he landed the contract for the shower curtain rings provision for the US Navy, before realising he might be annoying Neal and pushing him several times to say that Del is being a blabbermouth. Initially, Neal refuses to do so - until his patience runs out and Neal tells Del that HE IS a blabbermouth. Del sits there looking hurt.

There is one deleted scene that you will find on the Blu-Ray extras and occasionally in the US TV showings (it's the only deleted scene that seems to have made it from the cutting room floor into the public domain) and it's beautiful. I'm grateful it made its way into the ether, but it just shows the audience just how much comedy gold must have been cut. We see the three passengers - Del, Neal and the elderly gentleman - at the window seat being served their inflight meals. The hard of hearing elderly gentleman was played by Bill Erwin. Hughes was a fan of Erwin's as he also played the grandfather in *She's Having a Baby* and a husband in the airport in *Home Alone,* whose wife convinces him to give their seats to Kate McCallister.

As the inflight food is served, Del had ordered a special - the seafood salad, whilst Neal has something that looks square and burnt. Del comments that seven hours ago it was a lasagne but with all the heating and reheating it now looks like that. Then he goes on to mention that his friend used to prepare the food: she lost the tip of their finger in the carrots, served on a flight to Singapore. Neal gives his lasagne to Del after he's been put off trying it and Del gives Neal's bun and salad to the elderly gentleman, who then also requests Neals' brownie. At this point, Neal protests. According to Del talking to the gentleman, *"He won't give you the brownie, he has a sweet tooth"*, before the passenger in front flicks her extremely long hair over Neal's brownie. Of course, Del and the elderly gentleman get to share the dessert treat. Neal just can't catch a break.

"Six bucks and my right nut says we're not landing in Chicago"

Del really does have a way with words and indeed he is right, all flights to Chicago are diverted to Wichita due to adverse weather conditions.

The intended route in the map is depicted by the broken line.

At Wichita airport, Neal calls home to tell Susan about the diversion and she asks "What's going on?" Overhearing, Del comments, "Trouble on the homefront?" and gives Neal his motto, "Like your work, love your wife", following it up with a warning that all flights are going to be cancelled and that they are stuck in Wichita.

The deadpan Wichita Airport Representative, played by Ben Stein, announces that Flight 909 to Chicago is cancelled - followed by a wry smile, the sign behind him displaying flight information is showing 'Destination: Nowhere'. As it so happens, Stein is also another of Hughes' favourites, he played the economics teacher in *Ferris Bueller's Day Off*.

Neal's luck hasn't changed; he can't find a motel for the night, they are all booked up. Del comments, "You called home, I called the Braidwood Inn", and there is a glimmer of Neal's luck turning. Del suggests he can fix him up with a room. If Neal pays the cab fee he'll make sure he has somewhere to stay and looking around and seeing people sleeping on the dirty airport floor, Neal agrees.

Doobby's Taxiola

You will have seen Hughes regular Larry Hankin as Old Joe in *Breaking Bad* and Mr Heckles in *Friends* as well as Officer Bazlak in *Home Alone* and Hank in *She's Having a Baby.* His character in *PTA*, Doobby, is a rough diamond. Judging by Doobby's cab covered in Pin-up girl pictures, neon lights, chintz, novelty air fresheners and plastic dolls, he doesn't look like he takes customer care seriously. En route to the motel Neal asks what's taking so long, when Del asks why they haven't taken the interstate. Doobby replies that as Neal has never been there before they are taking the scenic route (even though it's the middle of the night).

A Short
From all the extra footage Hughes filmed for the Doobby's Taxiola scene, a 10-minute short was created.

In an interview with Hankin he recalled,
"I revered John (Hughes), I was very happy to work with him, he made great movies and this guy knew 'funny'. He was watching me and John (Candy) hang out and riff, so John Hughes set aside a whole afternoon of me, John and Steve Martin to work in the cab. The cab was set up on rockers in a garage, we weren't really driving around. When we shot the scene in the cab, the actual scene you saw in the movie took an hour to shoot. But then he sent everybody home except a very small crew, the cinematographer, the sound guy, him, Steve Martin, me and John.

"So for the rest of the afternoon we improvised in that cab for hours. It was really great because John and I were (from) Second City, so we were great at improvising, we were just playing together. We must have improvised for three hours just inside that cab. He (Hughes) was watching on the screen and he would come down and would just watch all three of us improvise and he would sit on this orange crate outside the cab, and he would say 'Remember Steve when you said that? and Larry, you said that and John you answer…', I was like this guy is incredible he has a photographic memory. So that was just really cool, I got to riff with two of the heaviest guys in comedy, for hours! None of that stuff ever appeared in the movie.

"A while later I was working with Chris Columbus on *She's Having a Baby* and I was talking about John with Chris Columbus and he said, 'Well yeah, I really respect your work Larry, especially that film short you did in the taxi cab.' I said 'What taxi cab?' He said, 'You know that one with you, Steve Martin and John Candy, you were playing Doobby in that film short.' I said, 'I didn't do any film short', he said, 'Well I was at John Hughes' house and when we were talking about doing this movie and he showed me the film short of you, Candy and Martin in the cab.' It was a ten-minute film. So that is what John Hughes did with that afternoon of improvising. I have never seen it."

Welcome to the Braidwood Inn

Location: Braidwood Inn - about 45 miles S/W of Chicago, was a Days Inn, now known as The Sun Motel, 140 South Hickory Street, Braidwood

Doobby's Taxiola rolls up at the Braidwood Inn. Del is delighted to make it but Neal doesn't look so sure (just like Martin in real life - Neal is a bit of a germaphobe). It looks cheap and unsavoury.

Welcoming enough proprietor, Gus Mooney (Del's friend and client - he sold him shower curtain rings), asks Del how he is and Del replies with one of his classic lines: "I'm still a million bucks shy of being a millionaire". Gus tells the odd couple that he only has one room left and it's a double. Neal hesitantly pays for it and when they enter room 114, it literally is a double - a small double bed, 70s in style and certainly in need of an update and a good scrub. They both look at the bed before Del asks Neal if he'd like to take a shower. Of course, he has to reiterate he didn't mean they take a shower together, so would Neal like to go first...

Neal gets into the shower, and as per usual has an unfortunate time. The water goes off, the shampoo stings his eyes, and when the hot water returns, it scalds him. Meanwhile, we see Del making himself at home, unpacking a few things, including a picture of his wife, Marie, that he carries everywhere, smoking a cigarette, watching TV and turning on the bed vibrator. By the time Neal steps out of the shower he sees a trail of destruction. There are wet towels everywhere, a newspaper on the floor by the toilet, lotions, vitamins, antacid liquid and potions all spread across the bathroom sink. The only dry towel-like object is a washcloth that Neal reluctantly uses.

Deleted scenes and script changes

The scene with Gus, Del and Neal initially played out a little differently. When Del asks Gus how he is, Gus replies;

Gus: I was doing pretty good there for a while but Sunday I pissed my pants during '60 minutes' so I guess I've gotta go back in for more plumbing work. I got your room all ready for you." Gus has other great lines, whilst explaining he didn't have a spare room for Neal he says, *"You know, Del, I'd rather shoot arrows out my ass than disappoint you or a friend of yours but I'm booked solid. I got three of those fat gals sharing a single as it is. One twin and two cots and them cots are really built for youngsters."*

It's at this stage Del suggests sharing, because after all, Neal had paid for the cab - Neal declines but is finally convinced and Del tells Neal he can pay for the room so he doesn't feel like he's being an imposition.

In the final shooting script, Gus goes on to tell them that someone died in their room last night and he had to bring a mattress in from his brother's. The dead man is Fritz Obermann - Del is upset, he knew him. Neal is more concerned that whatever killed him was contagious - according to Gus, poor old Fritz Obermann blew up, just blew up!

During the bathroom scene, what we don't see because it was cut out of the final edit, is that Del has obviously been using the rest of the bathroom whilst Neal was in the shower. In fact, in the official movie trailer, there is a clip of Del in his pyjamas, singing Elvis songs into the bathroom mirror using a hairbrush as a microphone. It is also Del's fault that the shower runs cold on Neal. Another cut scene shows Neal noticing in horror through the shower curtain that there is a shadow of Del sat on the toilet!

Del also takes delivery of a pizza, but he only has a 100 dollar note, so he has to go into Neal's wallet. The pizza is 9 dollars or 19 dollars depending on which script revision you read, Del hands over 10 or 20 dollars and tells the delivery guy to keep the change - the delivery guy is not impressed with such a measly tip.

Del tucks into the ugliest looking pizza you've ever seen, whilst watching TV on the vibrating bed.

When Neal gets out of the shower he complains to Del about the state of the bathroom and the fact that he used all the towels and most of the toilet paper! Del apologizes and blames the fact that he's a big guy and they are small towels, and regarding the toilet paper it's the New York hotdogs fault.

Neal wanted a salad, but the pizza place doesn't serve salads, so Del ordered his pizza with extra vegetables and saved him a slice. Then, on opening a warm beer each there is a double explosion as they've been sat on the vibrating bed (as mentioned but not seen in the film).

I like me...

Eventually, the pair get into bed, Neal moaning about his side being wet with beer, but not wanting to swap, he just wants to go to sleep. Fine by Del. But of course, many of us have our quirks and bedtime routines, for Del it's making sure he cracks his knuckles, then his neck, scratches his balls and then clears his sinuses. What follows is a hilarious scene of John Candy making the most horrific sounds, snorts and grunts, with a small 'sorry' in there too. As he continues poor Neal loses his cool and leaps out of bed - Del sticks up for himself, and Neal starts a tirade of anger and abuse of Del.

Neal: "You got a free cab, a free room, and someone who will listen to your boring stories. Didn't you notice on the plane when you started talking, I started reading the vomit bag? Didn't that give you some clue that this guy's not enjoying it?"

"Everything's not an anecdote. You have to discriminate. You choose things that are funny or mildly amusing or interesting. You're a miracle. Your stories have none of that. They're not even amusing accidentally."

"'Honey, meet Del Griffith, he's got some amusing anecdotes. Here's a gun so you can blow your brains out, you'll thank me for it.' I could tolerate any insurance seminar. For days, I could listen to them go on and on. They'd say, 'How can you stand it?' And I'd say, 'Cause I've been with Del Griffith, I can take anything.' You know what they'd say? 'I know what you mean. The shower curtain ring guy.'"

"It's like going on a date with a Chatty Cathy doll. There should be a string on your chest that I pull out. Except I wouldn't pull it out, you would! Ah! Ah! Ah! Ah! (whilst miming pulling a string out of his chest. By the way, when you're telling these little stories, here's a good idea... Have a point, it makes it so much more interesting for the listener."

To which, whilst looking incredibly hurt, Del gives a killer reply; "You want to hurt me? Go ahead if it makes you feel better. I'm an easy target. Yeah, you're right. I talk too much. I also listen too much. I could be a cold-hearted cynic like you, but I don't like to hurt people's feelings."

"Well, you think what you want about me. I'm not changing. I like--I like me. My wife likes me. My customers like me. 'Cause I'm the real article. What you see is what you get."

At this point Neal looks remorseful, Del gets back into bed and checks over his shoulder to see if Neal is still there. Neal gives up and goes to bed.

In all the excitement and exhaustion they must have slept pretty well as in the middle of the night a young man in a cap breaks into their room, goes through both of their wallets and steals their cash.

In the morning, Patsy Cline's *Back in Baby's Arms* is playing in the background. The camera pans over from Del's side table where you'll see the picture of Marie, some rubbish, Chiclets (candy-coated chewing gum), Cracker Jack popcorn, smokes etc. to Del spooning Neal. As cosy as can be, Del gently kisses Neal's ear, whilst Neal holds Del's hand.

This leads to one of the most famous lines in the film... Neal asks Del why he just kissed his ear? Del asks Neal why he's holding his hand? Neal asks Del where his other hand is?, Del says 'Between two pillows', to which Neal replies, "THOSE AREN'T PILLOWS!" before they both leap out of bed and try to cover their faux pas up with manly talk.

To finish off his perfect stay, Neal retreats to the bathroom in a sleepy state. He washes his face in the sink not realising Del's socks are soaking in there, then reaches for a towel and dries his face with Del's underwear!

The film cuts to Mrs Page, then to the outside of the Page's home. Mrs Page, as we know her best, or Susan to her husband, seems a little plain Jane. Trying her best to look after her family, her house is spotless, her children are well behaved, her Thanksgiving feast a triumph! However, her patience with her husband is wearing thin; you can tell she has to run the household alone, A LOT.

Neal and Del then go for breakfast where they make plans to get the train from Wichita but when Neal goes to settle up the bill he realises all his cash has disappeared from his wallet. Because Neal knows Del went into his wallet to pay for the pizza, he immediately accuses Del of stealing his money. Del takes offence and tosses him his own wallet so he can count how much cash Del has, turns out that his wallet was also empty of cash and it dawns on them both that their money has been stolen.

Del observes that the thief only took cash and not their cards so they could charge their way home, Neal has a selection of cards, Del just has a Chalmers card - great for clothes and gifts but not much else.

Sitting outside the Braidwood Inn on Del's trunk, they both wait for their lift. Gus has helped them out and asked his son to pick them up and take them to the station.

A rundown pickup truck arrives and Owen, Gus' son, who has the vibe of a redneck, steps out. Without saying a word, Owen, who is played by Dylan Baker (who would incidentally work with Candy again in the film *Delirious*), sizes the pair up, then spits.

Del: *Are you Gus' son?*
Owen: *I'm Owen. Are you the Shower Curtain Ring fella?*
Del: *Yeah, yeah, Del Griffith*
Del gets up to shake Owen's hand
Del: *How are ya? This is Neal Page from Chicago*

Owen spits and then wipes his mouth and saliva with his hand before shaking Neal's.

Owen then informs that the train doesn't run from Wichita unless you're a hog or cattle - the people train runs from Stubbville. Saying that will be fine, Del and Neal go to grab Del's trunk to put in the back of the truck. Owen stops them before shouting at his wife to "get your lazy behind out here and put that trunk up in the back". Neal and Del refuse but Owen tells them that she doesn't mind, "She's short and skinny but she's strong, her first baby come out sideways, she didn't scream or nothing". Neal and Del hurry to put the trunk in the truck themselves.

Sitting in the back of the open-air truck on the highway, Del breaks it to Neal that Stubbville is a bit further than Wichita - like around 30-40 miles further, no more than 45 though, depending on which way he goes, it could be up to 70 miles! Neal, wishing he had remembered to pick up his gloves at the beginning of the movie, spots a pair in the straw they are sitting on - as he reaches for them an aggressive dog jumps out of the straw and guards the gloves. By the time they pull into Stubbville, they are both freezing and covered in frost.

Behind the Scenes and script changes
According to John Candy's stand-in at the Braidwood Inn, Bob Williams, the local paper had advertised for extras. Only 22 years of age at that time, Williams remembers, "Our local newspaper ran a story about how extras were wanted as the movie was going to be partially filmed in the area. They were going to use the train station in our town but we did not have enough snow so that location was changed. I sent in mine and my brother's application to be extras to the *Holzer Roche Casting Company* in Chicago and we found out the movie was going to be a Paramount production. I received a phone call about being an extra, so me and my brother showed up and when they saw me they thought I'd be good as a stand-in since John Candy and I were basically the same size etc."

As a stand-in Williams would substitute for John Candy when the crew were setting up lighting and angles for cameras, to make sure that when they brought the actors in the ambience and shot was set up correctly. Being a stand-in is different from being a body double as the stand-ins never actually appear on camera, but nonetheless, it's an integral role that can make life easier for the actors and crew alike.

According to Williams, The Braidwood Inn was as seedy as it looked! "The hotel itself was already a shady place in real life. Several of the rooms were completely covered in velvet so I'm sure prostitution took place in that hotel. We also noticed bullet holes in various walls throughout the building. As a joke, a lot of the extras that were huddled all together in a cafeteria waiting for something to do had dubbed the place 'motel hell'."

Martin would later joke in interviews that during the shower scene he caught athlete's foot! There is also further evidence backing up Williams' claims you can see on screen: if you look at the room Del and Neal stay in, you will see two grubby handprints on the wall over the bed.

During the bedroom 'Those Aren't Pillows!' scene, we know Martin and Candy did an awful lot of ad-libbing. There is a theory that Candy came up with most of the sharing the motel/bed scene as he'd had a similar experience to this when he was just 19 with one of his best friends at that time, Jonathan O'Mara. Candy had gone to Buffalo to try and join the Marines, O'Mara went along for the ride and to try and talk Candy out of trying, luckily for us an old knee injury meant he couldn't get past basic training. During that stay in Buffalo, O'Mara is convinced it influenced the whole Wichita motel scene in *Planes, Trains and Automobiles*, from the beer cans exploding, sharing a bed etc. Certainly, the "Those aren't pillows" line was not in the script, even though it's one of the most commonly used phrases taken from the film.

It was also initially Del telling Neal he had to fart when the lights went out that made Neal lose his shit, of course, the clearing of Del's sinuses certainly worked better and was arguably funnier (mainly thanks to Candy's performance).

Neal is in even more hot water than we realise in the film. Susan is getting angrier and more suspicious by the minute and in a phone call home she tells him off for sharing a hotel room with a stranger. As Neal is trying to defend himself on the phone he gets dressed into his grey wool suit - what he doesn't notice is that the arms and legs are now a few inches short. Cut to the coffee shop breakfast scene, Neal is annoyed - Del tries to explain...

Del: I had no idea they'd launder and starch your suit. You were thrilled this morning when the laundry came back. Remember, you thanked me for sending it out even though you didn't ask me to? You know, I think if you find the right place, they can stretch your suit out so it'll fit again. I personally don't invest in fabrics that can't bear up to a motel laundry.

Del, being sweet old Del, has also ordered breakfast for Neal. He gets him a Pony Express (a ground beef and gravy omelette). Neal wanted a grapefruit but Del had eaten the last one, Del passes over his oatmeal that he's not yet touched. After they find out they've been robbed, Del tries to get the bill down by telling the waitress he never received his oatmeal - he can prove it, you can't smell oatmeal on his breath! The waitress knows his game, she remembers handing him his oatmeal, mainly because before delivering she pulled out a hair from it that 'would make your armpit proud'. Neal turns green. Del tells her he works for the Department of Agriculture and after he threatens the possible loss of operating license, the waitress rips the check-up.

Bob Williams remembers them filming the scene with Owen, "Just like any movie, they took a lot of takes for even the smallest of shots. The scene where Steve goes to shake Owen's hand and Owen spits in his hand first was shot many times." To make that scene work, John Hughes told Dylan Baker to spit in his hand without Martin knowing it was going to happen, Martin's reaction on screen was very real. Williams continues, "They did film a scene for me, but it ended up on the cutting room floor, as they say. In the movie, you will notice an opening scene of the Braidwood Inn where there are some hogs in a field across the road. I was supposed to be the hog farmer and when a woman came out of the hotel, who was supposed to be a prostitute, they cut to me and I was supposed to make the sooie hog call sound as if I was calling the hooker."

Stubbville

Stubbville Station was shot in South Drayton, Buffalo, New York. They arrive on Pine Street at Railroad Street to catch the train.

Neal collects the train tickets and has to explain to Del that they didn't have two seats together. Del wants to meet in the bar, Neal says he's going to get some sleep. Del requests his address so he can pay Neal back for all the money he has spent, Neal says it's a gift and they part ways. Neal takes his seat next to a teen that is on her way home for Thanksgiving, he's already acting sweeter and friendlier, he seems softer than the man we saw at the beginning of the film, so maybe annoying but well-meaning Del is having an effect on him. Neal then goes to sleep.

The train jolts to a holt and awakens Neal. It's broken down, quelle surprise! Smoke is billowing from the train's engine.

Everyone is asked to get off the train and trudge across a frozen ploughed corn stubble field. Del is ahead, struggling with his trunk, Neal thinks twice about helping him before catching him up to share the burden. They have been told to walk a mile, mile and a half, and they will be taken to Jefferson bus station.

Deleted scenes and script revisions

In the film, Neal is thrilled to be free of Del as he settles into his train seat, and he stays Del-free until the train breaks down. However in script revisions Hughes had other ideas. The alternative was Del visiting the buffet car, grabbing some nuts and a beer and walking down the train until he finds Neal. Neal is sleeping and Del puts his briefcase under the seat and sits down next to him. Sweet Del, takes his coat and tucks it around Neal to make sure he is warm, carefully placing it so he doesn't drop his beer. All is well and Neal smiles in his sleep. Next minute the jolt from the train stopping awakens Neal and Del's beer has gone flying, landing on Neal's feet - soaking his shoes.

Your Mood's Probably Not Going to Improve Much

Location: Jefferson City Bus Terminal

Neal and Del are sitting on a bench at the bus terminal, next to an elderly man with a box of mice on his lap. Del acknowledges that Neal is in a pretty lousy mood, and asks if Neal has ever travelled by bus before, to which Neal shakes his head 'no', Del observes "Your mood's probably not going to improve much". And indeed it does not.

The bus is rammed, every seat is taken, crying children, trash, windows steamed up, everyone looks miserable apart from a young couple making out opposite Neal. Del comments that it's better than a movie on a plane. Neal gets caught watching and the young man says to him "Why don't you take a picture, it will last longer", much to Del's amusement.

Del decides that it's now time to break the news to Neal that their tickets are only good till St Louis.

Someone (possibly Del) has started a sing-a-long on the bus and the mood is a little lighter. Finishing one song, Del shouts out to see who has got a tune, Neal Page has got one and looks happy to be involved until he starts singing it. Neal chooses *Three Coins in the Fountain* originally sung by Frank Sinatra in a movie by the same title, the whole bus is silent and turns around and stares before Neal promptly stops singing. Del saves the day with a rendition of *The Flintstones* that everyone gets behind - almost certainly Candy's idea as he loved *The Flintstones* cartoon.

When they arrive at St Louis Bus Station, Del decides he's going to make them some cash. Optimistic and creative, he starts selling his shower curtain ring samples as exclusive earrings to unsuspecting members of the public. Flattering the ladies as he goes, it is clear he does have the gift of the gab when it comes to sales, he introduces himself as 'Del Griffith, American Light and Fixture Company - Jewellery Division'. He sells the rings as Diane Sawyer-autographed earrings, Czechoslovakian ivory, the Walter Cronkite Moonring, rings filled with helium so they are very light, autographed by baseball legend Darryl Strawberry, earrings that were originally crafted for the Grand Wizard of China (not originals of course, but replicas, very good replicas). Whilst Del is being entrepreneurial, Neal is trying to ring home, but no one answers as it's his daughter Marti's Thanksgiving pageant, where she proudly announces that she's thankful her dad is coming home for Thanksgiving.

With Del's selling skills they take their cash to the bus station restaurant for lunch.

Neal is regretful that he wasn't home for Marti's pageant, he says "I've been spending too much time away from home", Del replies, "I haven't been home for years". For a minute Neal thinks Del is serious, before Del just passes it off as a term of phrase.

They discuss their options. There are no flights available and every ticket is booked up because it's the busiest travel day of the year. Del even calls his friend at Eastern Airlines only to be told that there is no chance of getting a flight from St Louis to Chicago. Neal drops a bombshell that they should split up because getting home might be easier that way. Del is hurt and disappointed, he says his goodbyes and walks out of the restaurant.

Neal plans to rent a car and drive the eight hours home.

Deleted Scenes and Script revisions
Originally, in the earlier scripts, Del doesn't sell his shower curtain ring samples to make some cash. In one version he sells his AT&T calling card and in another, an old family heirloom, his father's watch. It's never really explained in the film why Del

wants to make some cash (seeing as they are charging their way home on Neal's cards), however, in the scripts he explains to Neal that he feels so bad about how the journey has been going, the very least he can do is buy him lunch.

What's also not seen is the anger that is building up between Neal and his wife. Susan is grilling Neal every time he phones to explain what's happening and why he's not home yet, but she's giving him a really hard time and is starting not to believe any of the facts he's telling her. In one script, as Neal tries to placate his wife, the call is as follows;

Neal: I'm in St Louis. Why? Because I've always wanted to tour the Anheuser-Busch Brewery. Come on, Sue.
(Pause)
I'm sorry. It's been hell. I got hooked up with this shower ring salesman. I told you about him last night. Every time I listen to him...
(Pause)
Why do I listen to him? Good question. I'm stuck. No money. Everything's booked-up. I'm in the bus station. I'm tired and hungry and I'm mad.
(Pause)
I want to get home. I can't fly in. I've tried every airline. There isn't a seat left on anything. This is the busiest travel day of the year.
(Pause)
I think I'll just rent a car and drive home. It's about eight hours. Honey, I can drive alone. I'm not that tired. I'm not driving home with Del. I don't care if he can share the driving, if I have him along, something'll go wrong. I know it. I don't trust him an inch.

You're Messing With the Wrong Guy (Gobble Gobble)

Neal is at St Louis Airport. He gets off the Marathon Bus and the driver tells him his car is in V-5. He gets off the bus with car keys and rental agreement and looks for his car, but when he gets to the space V-5 the plot is empty. He tries desperately to get the attention of the bus driver but his efforts are futile, the bus drives off and it is the final straw that breaks the camel's back. Neal throws his briefcase and rental agreement on the floor in a fit of rage. He has to walk three miles back to the airport in the freezing weather, snow on the ground, alongside the highway and across a runway. He is pissed off.

When Neal finally makes it back to the airport to the car rental kiosk, he looks like a madman with his tie tied around his head to try and keep his ears warm. He's cold, dirty, furious. He gets to the rental desk and the jovial Marathon Car agent is on the phone, talking to her family about Thanksgiving.

That agent is played by Edie McClurg, a wonderful character actor that appears in Hughes' *Ferris Bueller's Day Off*, *She's Having a Baby* and *Curly Sue.* McClurg has also played various roles in *The Richard Pryor Show*, character voices in *The Smurfs*, *The Little Mermaid*, *The Jetsons* and many other roles. In the documentary *Getting There Is Half the Fun: The Story of Planes, Trains and Automobiles*, McClurg says, "With John (Hughes) nothing is usual. We were actually shooting *She's Having a Baby*. They were having to work on a lighting thing and didn't want everybody to leave the set because they were trying to fix lighting on specific people. John comes over and hands me the script and says, 'Would you read this scene out loud?' I read both parts, the whole scene, and I handed it back to him. I don't know why, I think he's probably working on this script and he wants to hear it, so I read it and give it back to him. And then they call, ya know, like a month or two later and say, 'Well we want you to play this car rental woman in *Planes, Trains and*

Automobiles'. It was like, ohhh is that what that was about, I was auditioning, in front of everybody."

The crazed suit, Neal, is standing at the counter, and watching the agent on the phone he's getting angrier by the minute. The agent is talking to her sister about Thanksgiving (by now a pretty sore subject with Neal) and her jolly disposition and lack of urgency to deal with the customer in front of her tips him over the edge. What happens next is a scene where Neal lets out all the frustration that has built up and drops the F-bomb 18 times. This scene alone is the reason why the film was an R rating (15 in the UK), instead of a PG.

Edie McClurg recalls, (it was) "Totally scripted, John wrote everything except the Thanksgiving riff, in order to make Steve a little more angry I decided I would be on the phone when he came up to the counter doing a transaction for a car or something, that's when I did several takes. Then John leaned over and said, 'This time, just talk about Thanksgiving', and I just let fly."

The agent doesn't appreciate how she's being spoken to, and it's obvious he's messing with the wrong lady. When she asks Neal if she can see his rental agreement, he says 'I threw it away', she replies with 'Oh boy', he replies, 'Oh boy what', the agent, 'You're fucked!'".

Still not catching a break, the only other way to get home is to get a taxi all the way from St Louis to Chicago! Funnily enough, Neal's request at the taxi rank gets him a negative response and the taxi dispatcher suggests maybe he should get a flight instead. Neal, still riled, picks on the wrong guy and replies "If I wanted a joke, I'd follow you into the john and watch you take a leak". After some back and forth insults, the dispatcher has had enough when Neal describes him as 'standing there like a slab of meat with mittens', and hits Neal square in the face. Neal falls back onto the road, and a car screeches to a halt, narrowly missing Neal's head. Del steps out of the car and is surprised to see Neal.

The dispatcher barks at Del to move his car, to which Del shouts, "What is your problem, you insensitive asshole!" Del agrees to move his car, if the dispatcher helps Neal up - sadly for Neal the dispatcher agrees and picks him up by his genitals!

Deleted Scene, script revisions and behind the scenes
Neal endures the bus to the car rental lot to pick up his car. Whilst he's waiting, he talks to an elderly man who claims he also is having a terrible few days trying to get home for Thanksgiving. Neal says it can't be as bad as his story - it is in fact very similar but worse because this poor man also had to have his foot amputated on Thursday! Sat on a packed bus, between two nuns, the driver pulls up and shouts for Mr Page, gives him the keys and tells him it's for a red Mustang, space E-67. Neal wishes the driver a happy holiday - the driver snaps back that whilst Neal will be eating turkey, he will be working.

Ken Tipton was the owner of six very successful video rental shops in St Louis at the time of filming. Now when video rental shops first came out, Hollywood didn't like the idea of them as they thought they would lose them money. Turns out Hollywood was wrong and back then, video rental ended up bringing in more than three times the revenue of the movie theaters, so after a while Hollywood started to treat video rental shop owners very nicely. Tipton's distributor had mentioned to him that he was a friend of Hughes and that they were going to start shooting a film called *Planes, Trains and Automobiles* nearby. He asked Tipton if he would like to run a competition for his staff where they could win places as extras on the movie. So in fact a lot of the people in the background in the scene where Martin comes into the airport car park and also in his "I want my fucking car" scene in Lambert Airport are many of Tipton's staff, and of course Tipton also wanted in on the action.

"It was shot in the winter of 86, but we had some really weird weather that was messing things up on set. So the first Assistant Director (AD) came over with my distributor and I immediately hit him with "I've been a fan of John's forever and I always wanted to be an actor" I was a heavyset guy. I was really busting the chops of the first AD, he said well hey you are heavyset, you look a bit like John Candy's younger brother, how would you like to be John Candy's stand-in? I was like, "Hell yes!" I didn't know what it was but it sounded good to me.

"Basically what it is, all the snow you see in the scene is fake snow that they bought in - in a truck from Illinois where the snow hadn't melted yet. So basically they put this plastic tape on the ground, in the shape of a T it was called a marker. So I would stand there whilst they would set up the lights etc. in other words being a stand-in is boring, you just stand there, but it's helpful that you look like the actor as they can get the right light, sound readings, sound checks, so 45 minutes of setting this stuff up, they drag me out of place, John comes out of his trailer, does four minutes of dialogue, cut, John would be back in his trailer, then they would put me back on the marker to film another cut. They only had two cameras, so they would shoot a long master, then a medium, then they would go for an over the shoulder shot. So basically 8 hours of me standing on a yellow marker and not getting to meet John at all which was really starting to piss me off.

"So at one point we did break for lunch or dinner, this time I could go eat in the big people's tent. I could see Steve Martin and Edie McClurg, but John wasn't there. So I see a production assistant, loading up a tray and this PA must have weighed about 90 pounds and there was no way that the amount of food on this tray could have been for this PA. I had the idea that maybe this was going to John. So I followed the PA and they started heading towards the big trailers and sure enough heading for John's. So I thought what the hell and I interrupted the PA and said, "Hi I am Ken, I am John Candy's stand-in, John wants me to deliver his food for him" the PA doesn't know anything anyway, they are so low on the list, so if anyone tells them anything they'll do it. So the guy gives it to me and I ask which one is John's and he said, "The one that says 'John Candy'".

"I knocked on the door and I said "Here's your lunch Mr Candy", and he said "Oh come on in". So I went in and I said "this is a nice trailer, nice trailer", he was sitting over on the right hand side and there is a table and a couch area and he was looking over the script of what he was going to be doing later that day. So I set it all down and said, "Hi my name is Ken Tipton", he says, "Hi", I say, "I'm your stand-in for today", and he says, "Oh how are you liking it?", "Oh yeah it's fine, but it's not what I thought it would be, I thought I would at least get to meet you at one time." And you could tell at that point he was like 'Oh shit this guy's not going to leave is he?' So I don't remember what he said but it opened up to 'Oh yeah I'm from here and I'm an actor and do stand-up comedy and improv', then I slowly kind of sat myself down.

"Now I look back at it I realise what an asshole I was. This guy is a working actor, he's trying to learn his lines for his next scene and he has this doofus in front of him, yammering about this, that and everything, and I just sat there and rambled whilst he ate. And he's eating and looking at the script and he was so sweet to let me sit there and be a fool, it lasted a good twenty minutes if not longer. He finally put his script down and he's eating and he's looking at me and he says, 'Well you know Ken that's very interesting, you know what, you need to stop though, I get what you mean.' Then I said 'I've been an idiot I'm sorry', I have never been in this situation with one of your actual heroes sitting in front of you eating lunch and I tell him that what he does is what I would love to do. He said, 'If you've got the passion, if you've got the passion for doing it you just have to follow it, but more importantly you need to realise that this is hard, it's not just fun, it's a lot of hard work, there is a craft to it. Just like there is a craft to be carpenters and plumbers and everything else, there is a craft to acting, it's not something you just do, you've got to train for it, you've got to rehearse, you've got to practice. People have no idea how much work actors do at home and behind the scenes before they actually stand in front of a camera and deliver some lines, and all the other technical things, how to hit their marks right, make sure the key light is hitting them properly, that you're not blocking other people and that you're not talking over people, and on top of all that you have to give a believable performance.'

"So he gave me this little pep talk about how it's not totally what people think it is and he was so nice about the way he let me down, not let me down but brought me down, 'Ya know what I totally understand you, everybody starts from some place, I was in the same position as you, I started in Toronto and did this and that and grew', and luckily he's now getting to do what he loves to do. So with that we left on very cool terms, I thanked him, he said, 'Ya know if you ever get serious about your acting and you're in Hollywood give me a call, I'll see what I can do to give you some advice, so you don't make all the mistakes I made'. I thought, wow, that was cool, and it was so genuine the way he did it, now in Hollywood people say give me a call but they don't want you to, they just want to get rid of you, but you could tell he was actually genuine."

I had a feeling when we parted ways that somehow, someday, our paths would cross again

Now in the car, Del is driving, he jokes with Neal that he's never seen anyone been picked up by his testicles before and he's glad he didn't kill Neal with his car - Neal wishes that he had (in a very squeaky voice). He can't believe Del has managed to get a car, Del puts it down to 'going with the flow'.

They have swapped places and Neal is now driving. Del is messing with his seat trying to get comfortable, he goes back and forth in it until eventually, it breaks. Swap back for another part of the journey, Neal is asleep in the broken seat, Del is smoking, Ray Charles' *The Mess Around* comes on the radio. Candy does a great performance mime to the song, including pretending to play keys on the dashboard and a thumb saxophone. He throws his cigarette stub out of the window and it flies back in and lands on the back seat. Feeling hot Del wants to take off his parka jacket, as he tries he gets stuck and loses control of the car. Eventually after much panicking, he manages to spin and stop. Neal awakes, Del explains that they nearly hit a deer. What they don't realise is that Del has spun the car around and is now facing and inevitably driving the wrong way up the highway!

A car on the opposite side shouts at them, "You're going the wrong way!" Del thinks they want to race, they persist in shouting and Neal realises they are saying that they are going the wrong way, Del wants to know 'how do they know which way they are going?' All of a sudden the penny drops and Neal realises they are on the wrong side of the highway with two trucks coming directly for them. Trying to tell Del, Neal doesn't manage to get the words out in time and they are heading for, and very nearly sandwiched between the two trucks coming towards them. Neal looks at Del and he's turned into the devil, laughing maniacally. Del slams on the breaks, his trunk, strapped to the boot of the car, flies over the car and into the road, the pair have to prise their fingertips from the dashboard. The car has been sheared down both sides, the wing mirrors are destroyed and the trim is ruined.

They retrieve Del's trunk from the middle of the road and sit on it to rest.

There is a glow from behind them, Del looks round, Neal looks round, they both look round and realise the car is now on fire (Del's cigarette butt finally went up). There is a look of horror on Neal's face before he starts laughing. He's laughing because he thinks Del has finally done it to himself, Del laughs along too.

Neal goes serious again and starts to question how Del managed to rent a car without a credit card, Del's explanation that he gave the lady behind the counter shower curtain rings just doesn't seem to stand up. Eventually, Del confesses that he used Neal's Diners Club card - somehow it ended up in his wallet. Neal goes crazy! He accuses Del of stealing, Del denies it, it just showed up in his wallet - he thought it was 'kindness'. Neal wants the card back, Del can't give it to him as he's already put it back in Neal's wallet, which is presently on fire in the car.

Del has the audacity to ask Neal if he's mad at him, Neal can't take anymore and hits Del hard in the stomach. Karma gets Neal back as he trips over Del's trunk for the second time.

Deleted Scenes and Script Changes
Del has only been driving for thirty minutes into the trip before he asks Neal to swap for a bit because his back is hurting.

Over at Neal's house, Susan, the kids and both sets of Grandparents are having dinner, discussing how great Marti's poem was at her pageant and what a shame it was that her dad missed it. The phone rings, Susan picks it up - it's Neal calling from a Roadhouse payphone. The venue is loud, Neal is trying to explain that he's in some roadside joint in Southern Illinois. Del interrupts Neal and asks him for five bucks, Neal relents and gives it to him, he warns him that as soon as he's off the phone they are leaving. Susan is upset, she wants to know what's going on, why it's taking him so long to get home - John, his colleague, got home last night, Neal can't believe it! Susan insinuates that she knows he's having an affair and asks how Del is. Neal hasn't read between the lines and thinks it's a genuine question, she warns him that he better not have Del's panties in his briefcase when he gets home, Neal, still not twigging, replies "Funny you should mention that. I dried off my face with them this morning". Susan hangs up.

It's not explained in the script why Del wants five bucks, however, there is a deleted scene that features Debra Lamb.

Lamb is playing a stripper that interacted with Del. Sadly this was cut out of the final edit, but luckily for Lamb, as a speaking part, it did earn her the SAG (Screen and Actors Guild) card, meaning she is now a member of an American Labour union giving her status as a performer and protection with worker's rights .

At another road stop, in a cafe, they discuss their wives. Neal is concerned he hasn't seen Del phone Marie. Del brushes this off that just because Neal hasn't seen him call his wife, it doesn't mean he hasn't and that she has a complete understanding about the situation. Neal thinks Del is a lucky man because his wife is mad as hell. Asking Del for advice on how he keeps his wife understanding, Del replies, "It's real simple. I love her from sun-up to sundown and I make damn sure I don't leave her sight until I'm convinced she knows it. Marriage can be a pretty flexible institution if the two parties involved know without a doubt that the love they give will never be less than the love they receive. It sounds like a load of cornball crap but it works like magic."

Whilst in the cafe they are warned that another storm is on the way. Del wants to get a motel, Neal wants to carry on and sleep in his own bed once he's home. The irony here is if Neal had listened to Del at this point, they would have missed the incident that led to them being on the wrong way on the highway, being sandwiched between two trucks and the car being set on fire.

Two dollars and a Casio

Location: El Rancho Motel, 36355 North Highway 41, Gurnee, north of Chicago near Wisconsin border

They pull up to the El Rancho Motel in the burnt-out car, Neal is still seething with rage. Del is complaining that Neal could have killed him, "You know you could have killed me slugging me in the gut when I wasn't ready. That's how Houdini died ya know?"

Neal goes into the motel and asks for one room, Del thinks that maybe they should get their own rooms if Neal is still mad at him, Neal tells him 'to get his own room'.

The motel clerk, played by Martin Ferrero, who is most famous for being eaten by a T-Rex whilst sitting on a toilet in *Jurassic Park*, seems sleepy and uninterested.

Neal's credit cards are so burnt up the motel clerk simply states, "Er, those aren't credit cards". Neal decides to pay cash instead, the room is $42.50 but he only has $17. Realising he's getting nowhere he offers $17 dollars and a hell of a nice watch. He gets the room but he is told he can't use the telephone or the satellite TV.

Del, charming Del, also doesn't have the $42.50, he does, however, have $2 and a Casio watch that he tries to sell as if he's on a shopping channel. Sadly for Del, his offerings don't cut the mustard and he thinks he's going to have to sleep in the burnt-out car, with no roof, in the snow.

Stories
Martin Ferrero was only on set for a day to film the motel scene, he reminisces, "When I went on set that day, John (Candy) was chatting with all the crew and he was on set practically all the time, talking to people and being very

outgoing. He welcomed me in, he said 'I know we are working together'. Steve Martin wasn't on set a lot, he would do his part and then go back to his trailer.

"When I saw Steve and John work that day I noticed there was no improv at all, they didn't improvise, they stayed on the script and I asked him about it, John said, "No we don't do a lot of improv because John Hughes has written a script that is pretty tight and there is a rhythm to what he has written, if you were to begin to improvise you might waste a lot of time, it might be funny but you might be upsetting the rhythm, it's a heartfelt important movie and you need to stay on course."

At this stage, they were so far behind schedule Candy and Martin had agreed not to improvise anymore.

Ferrero recalled, "John pulled me off to one side and said, 'are you preparing anything for your character?' and I said 'I have a backstory, but I won't use it if we aren't improvising'.
I told John I had done a commercial for tacos where I had done my Jack Nicholson impression. So John said 'let's hear your Jack Nicholson impression' and I did it, and it cracked him up. He said 'You wanna try and sneak that in on a take?', I said 'I guess I could try' and he said, 'but you've got to mask it - don't make it too much like him else it will be just an impression - but the attitude was correct for the character and you should try that'. I said 'OK', on one of the takes I did try it, I snuck a little of it in at the beginning and that's the one John Hughes used. So it worked out really well.

"When they were wrapping up for the day, John said he was heading back to his trailer and he was going to watch the end of the Lakers Celtics game (the Los Angeles Lakers and the Boston Celtics), they were in the final playoffs and he said 'why don't you just come over to the trailer to watch it?', and I went over the trailer, he gave me something to eat, he would ask me questions about the Celtic and Lakers rivalry - he said he was really into hockey but he didn't know that much about basketball. I was very vocal throughout the game, John found it very amusing, it turned out to be one of the most important games in basketball history, it was the game where Magic Johnson took the hook over Kevin McHale in the last seven seconds, LA that night was ecstatic."

Motel Room No 6

Neal gets settled into his motel room, there are twin beds and it's as dated (if not more so) than the Braidwood Inn. However, this time Neal doesn't really notice, he's just happy to have a roof over his head and a bed to sleep in. He tries to ring home, then remembers he can't because the lock is still on the phone. Del sits in the car and talks to himself, well actually he talks out loud to his wife, Marie; he's remorseful that he's found someone he likes and caused them so much trouble. Poor Del blames himself and just wishes his wife was there with him, he looks tearful.

Neal looks out the window. He sees Del sitting in the car, getting covered in snow. He sighs. He goes to the door and says, "You're going to freeze to death out there", Del turns around to look at Neal. Red-faced, Del looks like a little boy.

They spend the evening drinking miniature bottles of liquor, eating potato chips (they're everywhere!) and laughing. Del says all he has to show for his life is a bunch of shower curtain rings, Neal says at the very least, he has a woman he loves to grow old with. Del says nothing, he just thinks. Neal says to Del, "You love your wife don't you?", Del replies, "Love... is not a big enough word, it's not a big enough word for how I feel about my wife". They make a toast, "To the wives!"

Neal also apologises for hitting Del, Del feels like he deserved it, Neal tells Del he's 'unique', Del jokes that unique must be Latin for asshole. You can see the friendship has come a long way, they understand each other a little more now and certainly, Neal seems a little more tolerant.

In the morning the car is stuck in snow and ice, they have to rock to it to try and get some traction. Del puts the car in reverse, Neal tries to push, the car shoots back and drives through the front window pane and wall panels of their motel room! Realising they need to get out of there quick smart, Neal jumps in and they speed off.

Deleted scenes and script revisions
In the final shooting script, Del and Neal get pretty profound. They talk even more about their wives, work, money and legacy, Neal trying to make Del feel better about his financial situation. Del seems down that his legacy when he dies would be just some shower curtain rings that didn't fall down.

Del: *What do you pull down a year?*
Neal: *I do okay*
Del: *You know what I claimed in income last year?*
Neal: *That means nothing. Any second-string player in the NFL makes more in a week than Van Gogh made in his lifetime.*
Del: *Van Gogh Textiles up in Buffalo?*
Neal: *No, the painter.*
Del: *Oh*
Neal: *Money's no measurement of worth. True worth. Worth to the human race. I know because I have a lot of it and don't feel like I'm worth any more than when I was broke. In fact, I probably felt better about myself when I was broke.*

Neal asks Del if he's going to have a smoke before bed. Del can't, they were all burnt up in the car. Neal asks him to consider quitting, Del replies that his wife used to say that, Neal asks when she stopped, Del answers "Eight years ago, March".

In the final shooting script, the room is freezing cold and there is a shot of Neal curled up freezing whilst Del, in the other bed, seems to have all the covers. In the morning Neal goes to clean his teeth and his toothbrush is frozen in the cup, icicles are hanging from the shower. Del awakes and tells Neal he took the liberty of washing Neal's shorts in the sink, he tells Neal to wring them out and he'll dry them with his hairdryer. Looking in the sink, Neal's shorts are frozen in ice.

Back on the road, Del is feeling guilty about Neal having to trade his watch for the room, so he tries to give him his Casio. Neal declines.

The Radio Still Works - Clear as a Bell

In much better spirits than yesterday, the pair are driving along the highway, happily singing *Blue Moon Of Kentucky*. A state trooper notices them and pulls them over. Everything in the car is melted, including the speedometer so Del has no idea how fast he was driving, however, the radio works as clear as a bell.

The state trooper is played by Michael McKean, who is probably most famous for writing and starring in *Spinal Tap*. He tells them their car is clearly not fit for purpose and he's going to have to impound the vehicle until it can be made safe for travel. Del tries to appeal to the trooper's better judgment but sadly his charm doesn't work.

Deleted scenes and script revisions
The scene with Michael McKean was cut really short. What you don't see is the state trooper telling the travellers that they have actually overshot Chicago by 200 miles and they are actually on the Wisconsin state highway.

The state trooper finds their situation very suspicious and thinks they may be peddling drugs. He puts them both under arrest.

Location: Woodstock Courthouse, (which is now the Old Courthouse Arts Center), 101 North Johnson Street in Woodstock Illinois (also seen as the town of Punxsutawney from Groundhog Day).

Neal is standing outside the Courthouse. A large red truck approaches, sounding its horn. Del is in the passenger seat, he gets out and says "It's free and it's non stop", the driver is funny about having people in his cab, so they are in the back of a truck, which is refrigerated, sitting amongst boxes and boxes of cheese, Oshkonoggin cheese to be exact. Del comments that they will be in Chicago in around three hours. The more astute viewers will notice that Del is now sporting a black eye.

Deleted scenes and script changes
Originally filmed as Del and Neal leaving the Courthouse, Neal is limping a little. Because the state trooper is concerned they were selling drugs he has done an internal search on Neal, letting Del off when he found Neal was clean. Del then has to break it to Neal that because he was trying to save him some money, he neglected to take out insurance on the now burnt out, compounded rental car. At this point, Neal sees red again and socks Del in the eye.

Back to the truck driver, when he reaches his destination, he then tells Del and Neal to start unloading. Unbeknownst to Neal, Del agreed they would unload all the cheese in order for the free ride.

Hello Mrs Page

Location: LaSalle/Van Buren station, 121 W Van Buren St, Chicago, IL

Del and Neal are standing on the platform of LaSalle/Van Buren station: they have finally made it to Chicago. They reflect on their journey and laugh. Neal admits, after all is said and done, Del got him home. Neal's train pulls in. Del shakes his hand, he says how great it's been meeting him, Neal says Happy Holidays and embraces Del. They swap Thanksgiving greetings and Neal gets on the train. Del watches as the train departs, he is hurting.

Neal sits on the train, thinking of his family, the turkey. He then reflects on the things Del has said and done throughout his trip. Laughing at Del kissing his ear, the car setting on fire.
Del: I like me, my wife likes me

Neal: At the very least at the absolute minimum, you have a woman you love to grow old with

Neal: I've been spending too much time away from home.
Del: I haven't been home in years

Neal realises something is wrong.

The train pulls back into LaSalle/Van Buren.

Neal gets off.

He walks into the waiting room.

He sees Del.

He asks Del what he's doing there.

Del: I, I don't have a home. Marie has been dead for 8 years.

This cuts Neal like a knife.

Cut to a shot of Neal and Del carrying Del's trunk walking up the road to Neal's house.

Location: Oxford Road, Kenilworth, Illinois

They walk up to the house, Neal rings the doorbell, his daughter Marti answers the door and shouts 'DADDY!'

Neal introduces Del to his parents, parents in law and kids. His parents shout up to Susan to let her know Neal is home.

Susan comes down the stairs.

Neal	*Honey I'd like you to meet a friend of mine*
Susan:	*Hello Mr Griffith*
Del:	*Hello Mrs Page*

Susan and Neal embrace.

Del is thrilled, he squeezes his red mittens in his hands and smiles.

Everytime You Go Away plays out.

Deleted scenes and script changes
It was actually the test audiences that decided Neal would have the realization that something wasn't right with Del and go back for him, and that shot of the train pulling back into LaSalle/Van Buren is just the train leaving but in reverse.

Originally, Neal continues on his trip home, departing the train at Wilmette Subway Station. He walks into the station lobby, picks up a paper and trips over something - Del's trunk. Del is sitting on a wooden bench looking sheepish in the waiting room. Neal is angry, he can't believe he is here again. He nearly walks out, but stops himself and turns back, he asks Del what he's doing there.

Del eventually reveals that he doesn't have a home. Marie has been dead for eight years. Neal sits down and listens.

Del: She was sick when we got married. She just never got better. Once she was gone, I sold the house. I didn't much feel like being there. My life was empty enough as it was. I couldn't handle the thought of rambling around the place without Marie there so I just closed it up, took a few things and I've been on the road ever since.

Neal asks about the trunk, Del opens it up and shows him the remnants of his previous life.

Del: I didn't have much family. A brother in Montana, some cousins. Marie's folks died back to back the year after we married. They were pretty old. She was a late child. We didn't get the chance to have kids. She wanted three. Two girls and a boy.

Del goes on to explain how around 300 motels are his home, how he attaches himself to people, especially around the holidays, and this time he couldn't let go. What he really misses is giving himself to someone: not the getting, the giving. He apologizes and tells Neal he'll go back downtown, he's kept a tally of everything he owes and got his work address from his business card.

Back at the Page residence dinner is due to be served. Susan is upset and she has already told her parents that after Thanksgiving she will be leaving Neal. As she runs upstairs the doorbell rings.

Marti answers, Neal introduces Del to everyone. Susan is relieved. Basically, Del has just saved their marriage.

The closing shot is of them all around the dinner table. Del states that it's been a long time since he sat behind a turkey and gives thanks for being there with everyone, he says "I've always had a lot of things to be thankful for. But never more than right now." Neal agrees.

Marti starts saying the Pilgrim Toast for Thanksgiving, with some help from those around the table;

"Heap high the board with plenteous cheer, and gather to the feast,
And toast the sturdy Pilgrim band whose courage never ceased.
Give praise to that All-Gracious One by whom their steps were led,
And thanks unto the harvest's Lord who sends our daily bread"
-    *Alice Williams Brotherton*

The ending shot is of Del saying, "Amen".

The Soundtrack

Hughes loved music, he was an aficionado and prided himself on finding tracks others hadn't heard at that time. He especially loved English artists. Originally the soundtrack for *Planes, Trains and Automobiles* was going to be fully scored, so the pieces of music you hear when Del is struggling with his parka coat in the car was scored by Ira Newborn, along with other incidental music to portray the mood or what was happening in the film at the time.

Once Hughes had an edit of the film together, he sat down with his record collection and would play songs over the top of the scenes until he found tracks that he was happy with.

The soundtrack was released on LP, however, you'll notice from the track listing that there are some tracks that made the LP that you won't actually recognise from the film. Possibly from scenes that were cut. Other, very important tracks were not included in the soundtrack release, likely due to licensing issues.

The released soundtrack is as follows;
Release Date 1987
Duration 34:32
Original Soundtrack
Planes, Trains & Automobiles
Track Listing

1. *I Can Take Anything* [Love Theme from Planes, Trains & Automobiles] Andy Cox / John Hughes / David Steele / John Candy / Steve Martin
2. *Ba-Na-Na-Bam-Boo*, Westworld
3. *I'll Show You Something Special*, Balaam & the Angel
4. *Modigliani (Lost in Your Eyes)*, Jade Lee / Susan Ottaviano / Ted Ottaviano - Book of Love
5. *Power to Believe*, Gilbert Gabriel / Nick Laird-Clowes The Dream Academy

6. *Six Days on the Road* Earl Green / Carl Montgomery/ Steve Earle & the Dukes
7. *Gonna Move*, Dave Edmunds / Nick Lowe, Dave Edmunds
8. *Back in Baby's Arms*, Bobby Montgomery, Emmylou Harris
9. *Red River Rock*, Tom King / Ira Mack / Fred Mendelsohn, Silicon Teens
10. *Wheels*, Chris Hillman / Gram Parsons, Stars of Heaven

Amongst the songs that were omitted are;
Everytime You Go Away, Paul Young, covered by Blue Room
Mess Around, Ray Charles
Blue Moon of Kentucky, Bill Monroe
Continental Trailways Blues, Steve Earle
Lost Again, Yello

Other PTA Trivia

The Budget
Planes, Trains and Automobiles was made for $30 million and brought in $49.5 million at box office. $100,000 of that money was spent building the interior of the Pages' house and the production company was furious at the expense, especially considering how little of the house was used in filming.

Martin and Candy couldn't resist the script
The reason Hughes landed these two big hitters of comedy was because his script was so strong. Steve Martin had been looking to do a straight role and exceeds himself, he loved the 'Give me a fucking car' scene at the airport and was on board. For John Candy it felt like someone had got into his head and it was an immediate 'yes!'. With the casting of Martin and Candy, Hughes literally took their real personalities and amplified them within the script.

Martin later talked in interviews about his rapport with Candy, "At that point in my career, this was the direction I was headed for-more emotional roles. John Candy was one of the best acting partners I've ever worked with. We had great timing with each other".

Martin also told JC Corcoran in an interview that he thought *Planes, Trains and Automobiles* was some of Candy's finest work, "I saw him do scenes that aren't in the movie that were just breath-taking".

Martin remembers fondly "It was the first day of filming, he brought all this exercise equipment, jogging things, stationary bikes, weights and everything, and then never touched them!

"Well, he was a very sweet guy, very sweet and complicated. He was always friendly, always outgoing and funny, nice and polite, but I could tell he kind of had a little broken heart inside him", which was possibly one of the reasons he played Del so well.

Hollywood
Although most of the scenes were filmed in either Chicago or New York, filming of the interior of the plane and Doobby's Taxiola were actually filmed at Paramount Studios in Hollywood.

Martin thought the script was too long
Although Steve Martin loved the script, he thought it was going to be cut down from 145 pages to the usual 96 for a comedy movie When he mentioned this to a bemused Hughes, he suddenly realised that wouldn't be the case.

Marie wasn't just a picture
Beautiful Marie Griffith. In the film, we only know Marie as a picture her husband, Del, carries around with him. Every night he places her photo by his bedside. So by the end of the film we find out Del lost Marie eight years ago, however that picture is of actor Susan Issacs. There were actually flashback scenes filmed with Candy and Issacs that weren't used in the final movie. Would they have made us even more distraught when we finally found out Marie's fate? Regardless, Candy portrays Del's love for Marie beautifully and our heart breaks for him when the twist is revealed.

The Weather
The cast and crew experienced their own frustrations and *PTA*-style travel, driving from location to location to find snow. It was their quest to find the white stuff, along with all the ad-libbing that made them fall so behind schedule. In the end they had to ship snow in from Illinois.

No Planes, Trains and Automobiles

Production hit a snag when no actual travel companies wanted to be associated with the film for fear that it would affect their reputation. The team had to get round this by hiring 250 cars and a car park to create the car rental scene, as well as building a twenty mile stretch of railroad.

John Candy's perm

Steve Martin was pretty lucky in the costume department: his character just needed a suit, hat, briefcase, and a nice watch. John Candy had to be a little more creative and costume designer Marilyn Vance dressed him up in more clashing colours and patterns (including those fabulous pyjamas) - basically reflecting Del's sweet and eccentric personality. For the role of Del, Candy also grew a moustache and had to have his hair permed. The hair perming took place at Crimpers Haircutters in Buffalo, New York.

That Casio Watch

Del's Casio watch is model A159W and you'll find they are still available.

Del's Trunk

According to John's friend and radio producer, Doug Thompson, after filming, Del's trunk was kept in John's office in Brentwood and used as a coffee table.

Spencer Davis loved Martin's banjo playing

Doug Thompson was regularly on set with John Candy as they were writing shows for 'That Radio Show with John Candy'. Steve Martin used to hang out in Candy's trailer a lot. Thompson brought Spencer Davis down to set to see Candy, and Martin was there. Davis complimented Martin on his banjo playing, Martin just said, "I don't play anymore", to which Davis replied, "Pity". Luckily Martin reignited his love for the banjo later on.

Other stories from set

Greg Agalsoff was the boom operator on *Planes, Trains and Automobiles*: "I was certainly a fan of John's before we met and worked together. What made me a bigger fan was what I had heard of him by other crew members. Unlike other crew members who generally are introduced to the actors they will be working with on the first day of shooting, I was invited to have a beer with him in our hotel bar in Buffalo, NY, by John's driver and friend, Frank Hernandez. Several weeks earlier, when I ran into Frank on a studio lot and we both discovered that we would be working together, Frank told me that I would never work with a nicer person. He was more than right. When I met Frank and John in the bar, and was introduced, John was so very warm and unassuming. He smiled and said, "If Frankie says you're ok, then you're ok." A Buffalo Sabres hockey game was on the TV and I found out how rabid of a hockey fan John was!

"John got along with everyone. I mean everyone. He kept all of us 'in stitches' and both actors and crew alike adored him. John Hughes would have a most difficult time stifling his laughter in so many of the scenes that we did. Great to everyone, all the time, even when the situation was difficult.

"A great memory of John was when the great Chicago Blackhawk hockey player, Bobby Hull (aka the "Golden Jet") came by to meet John at a bar location we were shooting in. John was like a little kid, meeting his hero."

Agalsoff remembers the end scene at the train station, the most heartbreaking scene in the movie, he recalls, "My favorite memory of John was the day we were shooting at a small train station. We had been doing comedy for three months, and suddenly he was called upon to do a poignant, heart-wrenching scene. It was a side of him that I hadn't seen before, and I am tearing up when I think of the effort he put out (sic) and the incredible result we witnessed. When I saw the film, the edited version just didn't do to me what it did to all of us that day. John wanted so badly to get a juicy dramatic role. If I recall correctly, he went to do a reading for a very serious role, and was quite nervous about it. He was very disappointed when he didn't get the role.

"I didn't really hang out off set with John, but there was an occasion that stands out in my mind. While on location, he invited a large group of us over to his suite and made a huge pot of spaghetti and salad for everyone, with plenty of beer for all. We then watched a screening of a film that I believe he acted in, *Cannonball Run III*". You cannot beat John Candy's hospitality, his ability to look after people and make them feel comfortable was consistent."

Planes, Trains and Self Esteem - some Takeaway Life lessons

There are so many lessons we can learn from this beautiful film:

- Never race for a cab, it won't be worth it.
- Like your job, love your wife.
- Always tip the pizza delivery person.
- Always like yourself, and don't be a cold-hearted cynic.
- Never underestimate the power of a shower curtain ring when you are in trouble.
- *The Flintstone*s theme tune is always a good shout if you need to suggest a song.
- Never throw away your rental agreement.
- If you need to be home for an important event, leave early just in case!
- You never know what someone is going through, so be kind, always.

The legacy of *Planes, Trains and Automobiles* is strong. Played repeatedly at Thanksgiving and Christmas, this film never fails to touch our hearts and our funnybones. Hughes has always had a way of making his characters so real and bringing real empathy to the stories he tells, and this story is a timeless classic that we can all relate to. As the late film critic, Roger Egbert reflected in 2000, "Some movies are obviously great. Others gradually thrust their greatness upon us. When *Planes, Trains and Automobiles* was released in 1987, I enjoyed it immensely, gave it a favorable review and moved on. But the movie continued to live in my memory. Like certain other popular entertainments (*It's A Wonderful Life, ET, Casablanca*) it not only contained a universal theme, but also matched it with the right actors and story, so that it shrugged off the other movies of its kind and stood above them in a kind of perfection."

Empathy, unlikely friendships, luck (good and bad) and kindness are the order of the day. No other road trip film has come close in longevity or public love and let's face it, love is not a big enough word.

Those Aren't Pillows!

Bibliography

Books
Paul Hirsch, A Long Time Ago In a Cutting Room Far, Far Away…, 2020, Chicago Review Press
Kirk Honeycutt, John Hughes A Life in Film, 2015, Race Point Publishing
Tracey J Morgan, Searching For Candy, 2019, Kindle Direct Publishing

Script Revisions
John Hughes, Planes Trains and Automobiles, 22 May 1986
John Hughes, Planes Trains and Automobiles, Final Shooting Script, 23 June 1987

Documentaries
Getting There is Half the Fun: The Story of Planes, Trains and Automobiles

Films
Planes, Trains and Automobiles, John Hughes, Hughes Entertainment, Paramount Pictures, 1987

Websites
www.rogeregbert.com
www.imdb.com

Interviews
Jonathan O'Mara
Larry Hankin
Ken Tipton
Bob Williams
Greg Agalsoff
Martin Ferrero
Doug Thompson

Much love and thanks go to Rhys Perry, Joe Shooman, Gary McGarvey/Horse, David Morgan, Derek Morgan, Mum and Rich, Elle Howells, Steve Swain, Lee Moore, Steven Elliott, Jason Swoboda and Johnny Zito.

Huge appreciation and thanks to those who gave me their time and memories via interviews; Jonathan O'Mara, Larry Hankin, Ken Tipton, Bob Williams, Greg Agalsoff, Martin Ferrero and Doug Thompson

About the Author

Tracey J Morgan lives in Shropshire, UK, with her boyfriend and clowder of rescue cats. Born in the late 70s, Morgan is a huge fan of 80s movies and John Candy. She has worked in the creative industries as a music artist manager, promoter, record label owner and DJ. She loves her allotment, making jam, listening to music, kitchen dancing, and she daydreams - a lot.

Those Aren't Pillows! is her third book.

Other titles by the author;
Searching For Candy, John Candy: A Biography
The A to Z of John Candy

SeaRcHiNG
FOR
CaNDY
bY TRAceY J.
MORGaN

JOHN CANDY : A BIOGRAPHY

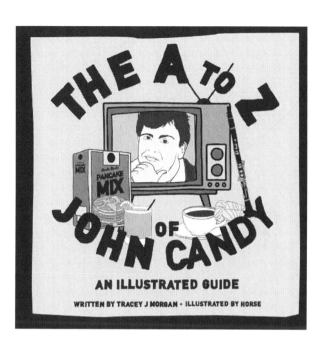

THE A TO Z OF JOHN CANDY

AN ILLUSTRATED GUIDE

WRITTEN BY TRACEY J MORGAN · ILLUSTRATED BY HORSE

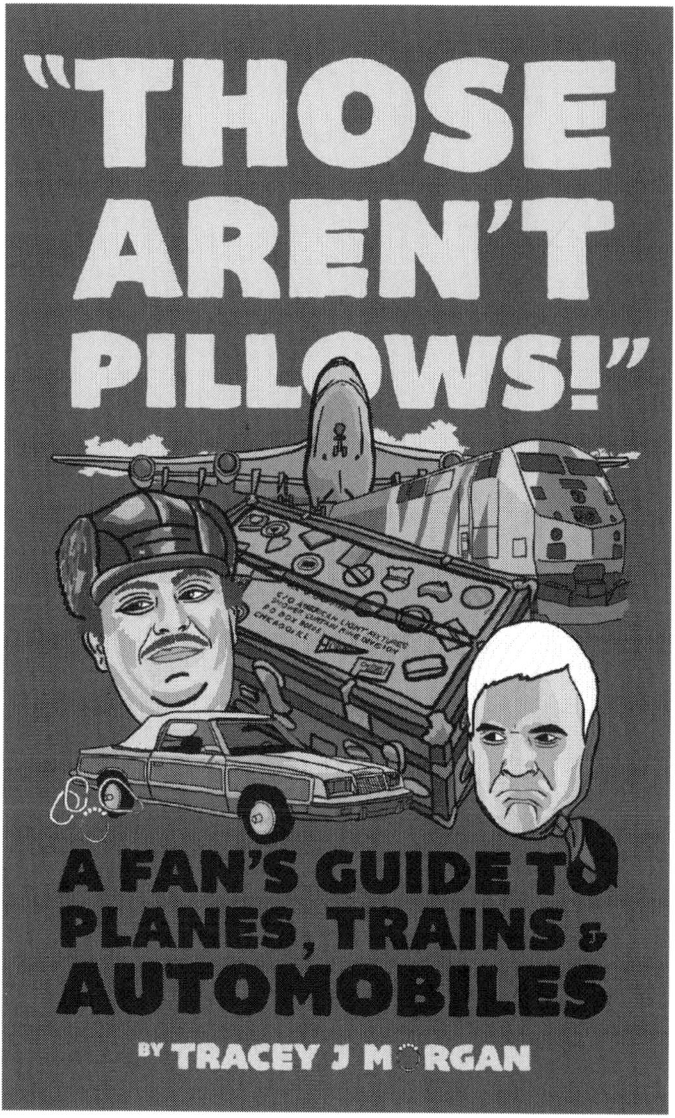
"THOSE AREN'T PILLOWS!"
A FAN'S GUIDE TO PLANES, TRAINS & AUTOMOBILES
BY TRACEY J MORGAN

Printed in Great Britain
by Amazon